NATIONAL GEOGRAPHIC | **GLOBAL ISSUES**

HEALTH

Andrew J. Milson, Ph.D.
Content Consultant
University of Texas at Arlington

Acknowledgments

Grateful acknowledgment is given to the authors, artists, photographers, museums, publishers, and agents for permission to reprint copyrighted material. Every effort has been made to secure the appropriate permission. If any omissions have been made or if corrections are required, please contact the Publisher.

Instructional Consultant: Christopher Johnson, Evanston, Illinois

Teacher Reviewers: Heather Rountree, Bedford Elementary School, Bedford, Texas

Photographic Credits

Front Cover, Inside Front Cover, Title Page ©Tim Gainey/Alamy. **4** (bg) ©Danita Delimont/Gallo Images/Getty Images. **6** (bg) ©Thomas Coex/AFP/Getty Images. **8** (bg) Mapping Specialists. **10** (bg) ©Irene Abdou/Alamy. **13** (bg) ©Jake Lyell/Alamy. **14** (t) ©REUTERS/Handout Old. **16** (bg) ©BOGDAN CRISTEL/Reuters/Corbis. **19** (bg) ©Daniel Mihailescu/AFP/Getty Images/Newscom. **21** (bg) ©Daniel Mihailescu/AFP/Getty Images. **22** (bg) ©Feliciano dos Santos. **23** (tl) ©Feliciano dos Santos. **24** (br) ©Feliciano dos Santos. **25** (bg) ©Feliciano dos Santos. **27** (t) ©St Petersburg Times/James Borchuck/The Image Works. **28** (tr) ©jo unruh/istockphoto. **30** (tr) ©Laurence Mouton/PhotoAlto/agefotostock. (br) ©jo unruh/istockphoto. **31** (tr) ©Jake Lyell/Alamy. (bg) ©Duncan Smith/Photodisc/Getty Images. (br) ©Scott Camazine/Alamy. (bl) ©Science Picture Co/Science Faction/Getty Images.

For permission to use material from this text or product, submit all requests online at www.cengage.com/permissions.

Further permissions questions can be emailed to permissionrequest@cengage.com.

Visit National Geographic Learning online at www.NGSP.com.

Visit our corporate website at www.cengage.com.

Printed in the USA.

RR Donnelley, Jefferson City, MO

ISBN: 978-07362-97745

12 13 14 15 16 17 18 19 20 21

10 9 8 7 6 5 4 3 2 1

Pictures of HEALTH

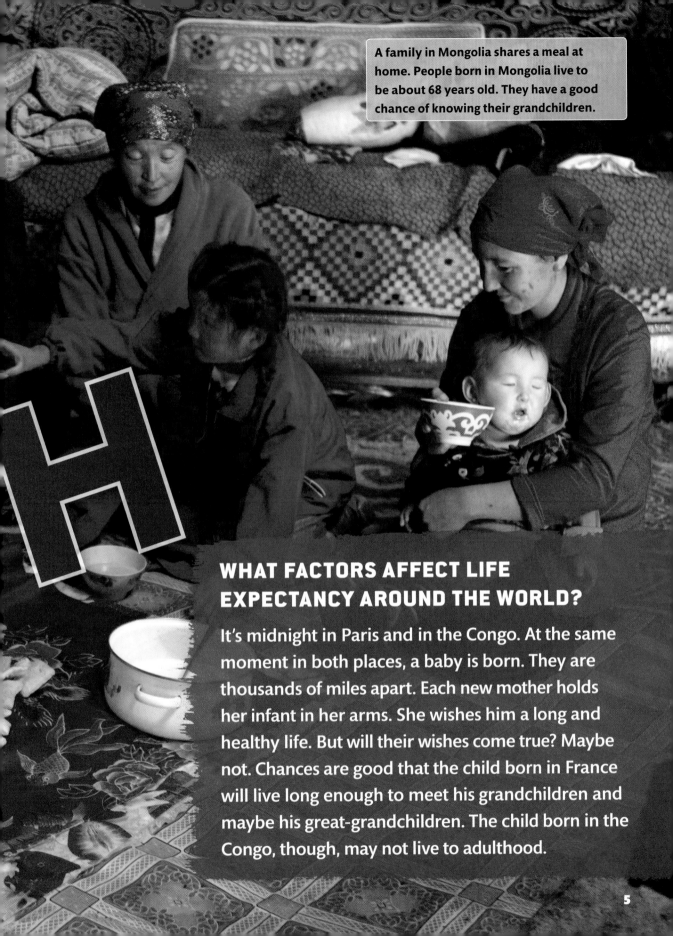

A family in Mongolia shares a meal at home. People born in Mongolia live to be about 68 years old. They have a good chance of knowing their grandchildren.

H

WHAT FACTORS AFFECT LIFE EXPECTANCY AROUND THE WORLD?

It's midnight in Paris and in the Congo. At the same moment in both places, a baby is born. They are thousands of miles apart. Each new mother holds her infant in her arms. She wishes him a long and healthy life. But will their wishes come true? Maybe not. Chances are good that the child born in France will live long enough to meet his grandchildren and maybe his great-grandchildren. The child born in the Congo, though, may not live to adulthood.

WHO WILL LIVE? FOR HOW LONG?

Health is a basic human concern. We all want to be healthy regardless of who we are or where we live.

One way of looking at health is through **life expectancy**, or the average number of years a person can expect to live. Not everyone has the same life expectancy. A person born in Spain, for instance, has an average life expectancy of 81 years. In Nigeria, though, life expectancy is just 52.

Why do these inequalities exist? Why are the chances for a long and healthy life so different around the world?

In this book, you'll read about some factors that influence life expectancy. Health is about more than just lifestyle and **heredity**, or the genes people inherit from their parents. It isn't even only a medical issue. Health is a reflection of society, including culture, politics, economics, and access to **health care**—that is, medical services.

This laboratory in France makes a medicine to prevent H1N1, a severe type of flu that can spread very quickly. Medicines such as these are expensive to manufacture and distribute and can be slow to reach remote or rural areas of developing countries.

OUTBREAKS AND BREAKTHROUGHS

Health has become a global issue. Diseases can cross borders. A **virus** is a tiny organism that infects living cells with disease. One of these can erupt in Malawi on Monday and can be in New York or Tokyo by Tuesday.

Scientific discoveries cross borders too. Sometimes it takes a team to solve a medical problem—including experts from around the world combining knowledge and resources.

Scientists still don't understand many of the factors that influence life expectancy. What explains the clusters of elderly people around the world who live healthy lives into their 90s? How do they stay so healthy for so long?

There are no simple solutions to health problems around the world. For example, wealth does not always guarantee good health. One measure of a country's wealth is **GDP per capita**, or the value of the goods a country produces per person. However, GDP per capita is not necessarily linked to life expectancy. Other factors may be more important to good health, such as a balanced diet, regular exercise, and being part of a strong community.

The good news is that we can advance good health everywhere on Earth. Two countries that are confronting health issues are Nigeria, in Africa, and Romania, which is in Europe. Both countries show that positive steps can be taken toward improving health.

LIFE EXPECTANCY AND INCOME

	LIFE EXPECTANCY	GDP PER CAPITA	LEADING CAUSE OF DEATH OR ILLNESS
Japan	84 years	$34,000	Stroke
France	81 years	$35,000	Cancer
United States	78 years	$48,100	Coronary heart disease
Mexico	77 years	$15,100	Coronary heart disease
Brazil	73 years	$11,600	Coronary heart disease/stroke
India	67 years	$3,700	Coronary heart disease
Russia	66 years	$15,700	Coronary heart disease
Kenya	63 years	$1,700	HIV/AIDS

Sources: *CIA World Factbook*; World Health Organization, 2012

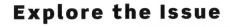

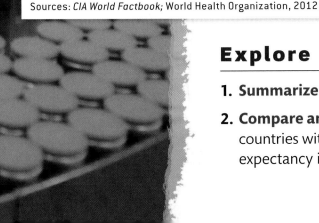

Explore the Issue

1. **Summarize** Why is health a global issue?

2. **Compare and Contrast** How does life expectancy in countries with a high GDP per capita compare with life expectancy in countries with a low GDP per capita?

WORLD Hot Spots
Health Concerns

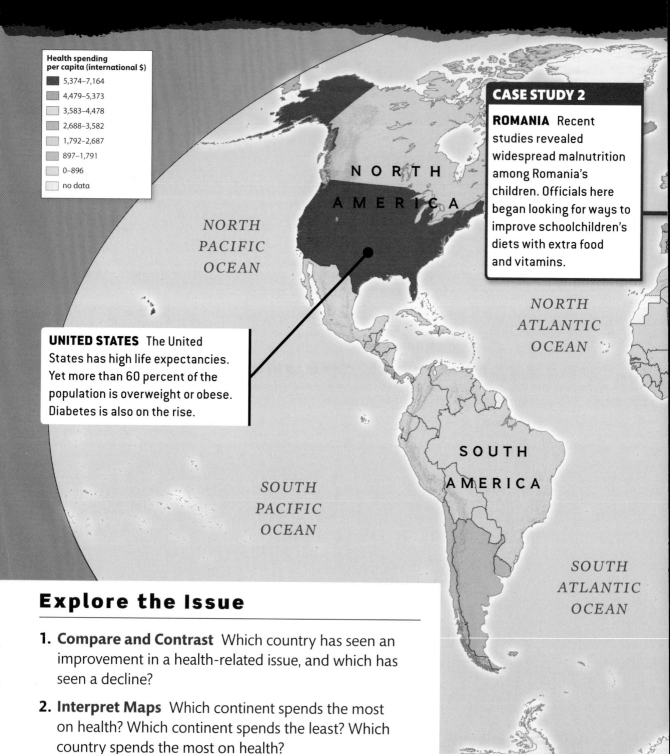

Health spending per capita (international $)

- 5,374–7,164
- 4,479–5,373
- 3,583–4,478
- 2,688–3,582
- 1,792–2,687
- 897–1,791
- 0–896
- no data

NORTH AMERICA

NORTH PACIFIC OCEAN

SOUTH AMERICA

SOUTH PACIFIC OCEAN

NORTH ATLANTIC OCEAN

SOUTH ATLANTIC OCEAN

CASE STUDY 2

ROMANIA Recent studies revealed widespread malnutrition among Romania's children. Officials here began looking for ways to improve schoolchildren's diets with extra food and vitamins.

UNITED STATES The United States has high life expectancies. Yet more than 60 percent of the population is overweight or obese. Diabetes is also on the rise.

Explore the Issue

1. **Compare and Contrast** Which country has seen an improvement in a health-related issue, and which has seen a decline?

2. **Interpret Maps** Which continent spends the most on health? Which continent spends the least? Which country spends the most on health?

Study the map to learn about health concerns in different parts of the world.

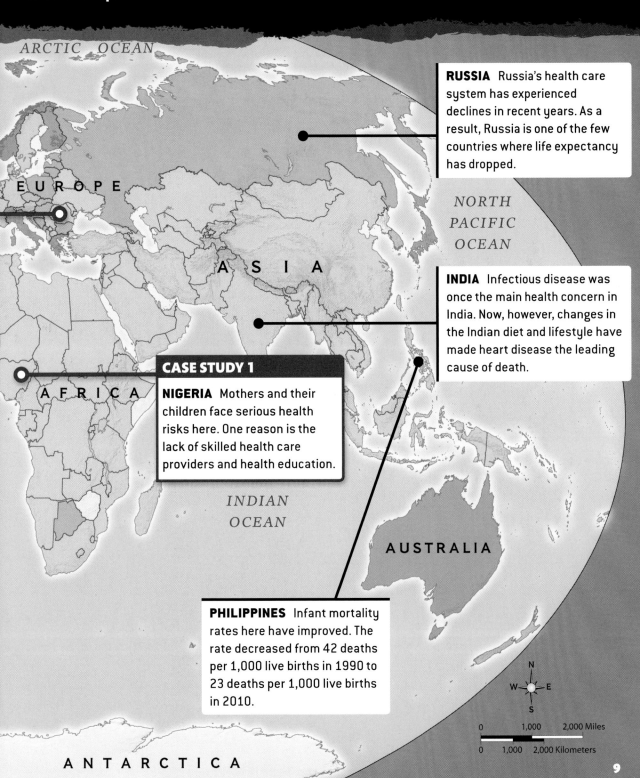

RUSSIA Russia's health care system has experienced declines in recent years. As a result, Russia is one of the few countries where life expectancy has dropped.

INDIA Infectious disease was once the main health concern in India. Now, however, changes in the Indian diet and lifestyle have made heart disease the leading cause of death.

CASE STUDY 1

NIGERIA Mothers and their children face serious health risks here. One reason is the lack of skilled health care providers and health education.

PHILIPPINES Infant mortality rates here have improved. The rate decreased from 42 deaths per 1,000 live births in 1990 to 23 deaths per 1,000 live births in 2010.

ARCTIC OCEAN

EUROPE

ASIA

AFRICA

NORTH PACIFIC OCEAN

INDIAN OCEAN

AUSTRALIA

ANTARCTICA

N
W E
S

0   1,000   2,000 Miles

0   1,000   2,000 Kilometers

Mothers and Children AT RIS in Nigeria

The mosquito net hanging above the bed protects this mother and her children from mosquitoes that carry disease.

THE HEALTH OF BABIES

Justinah Chukwudi (CHUK-wud-ee), who lived in a small village in the African country of Nigeria, knew she was very lucky. She was expecting her fourth child. One day she was visited by a Health Ranger, a government worker whose job was to check on the health of young mothers and children. The Health Ranger saw that Justinah had very swollen ankles and other signs of a difficult pregnancy. Acting right away, he arranged for Justinah to get a hospital scan. The scan showed Justinah was carrying not one baby, but three!

Then the Health Ranger made sure that Justinah was admitted to a hospital. There, she delivered healthy triplets. Because of the Health Ranger's quick action, Justinah felt confident that her babies would grow into healthy children.

Justinah's country of Nigeria is a **developing nation**, meaning that it has a low income per person. Developing nations face a major challenge to improve the health of mothers and young children. If developing nations can meet this challenge, they can dramatically improve the standard of living of their populations.

NIGERIA'S CHILDREN AT RISK

Although people such as the Health Rangers bring hope to Nigeria's villages, the country faces serious health challenges. Tragically, thousands of children do not live to see their fifth birthday. They are the victims of diseases such as pneumonia and measles. One particular problem is **malaria**, which is a disease carried by mosquitoes. In Africa, this disease is responsible for 20 percent of all childhood deaths.

Another cause of poor health among Nigeria's children is **malnutrition**, or the lack of healthful food. Many of Nigeria's children do not have enough fruits, vegetables, and other foods with **nutrients** that allow them to develop healthy bodies.

The lack of even one key nutrient can cause malnutrition in children. This condition requires treatment. In most cases, malnutrition can be corrected by adding nutritious foods to a child's diet. However, if the condition goes untreated, it can lead to mental or physical disabilities.

THE HEALTH OF MOTHERS

The health of children is closely connected to the health of their mothers. One particular challenge is helping more mothers survive childbirth. Maternal mortality is the death of a woman from causes due to pregnancy or birth. In many parts of the world, maternal mortality is a major health concern. The United Nations (UN) estimated that during every minute of the year 2000, a mother somewhere in the world died during childbirth. Nearly all those deaths were in poor countries.

Other factors contribute to poor health in young women. In societies where a woman's main role is to have children, girls sometimes get married very young. As a result, they do not receive an education and do not develop the skills to become employed. They also may not receive as much nutrition as boys while growing up. As a result, they don't know how to take good care of themselves. These girls may also have babies at a young age.

HOPE FOR MOTHERS AND CHILDREN

Under these conditions, young women often deliver low birthweight babies, meaning that the babies are born small and thin. Low birthweight babies are less likely to survive and grow into healthy children.

In spite of these challenges, though, hope has begun to take root in sub-Saharan Africa. The United Nations International Children's Emergency Fund (UNICEF) has set high goals for improving mothers' and children's health. Research shows that the answer is not expensive medicine or new technology. The best way to improve the health of mothers and children is to provide them with skilled health care.

NIGERIA BY THE NUMBERS

13.8%	Chance a Nigerian child will die before age 5
0.8%	Chance a child in the United States will die before age 5
25.5%	Children in Nigeria underweight at age 0–6 months
2.8%	Children in the United States underweight at age 0–6 months
5.2%	Portion of GDP spent on health in Nigeria
13.0%	Portion of GDP spent on health in the United States

Source: World Health Organization, 2004–2009

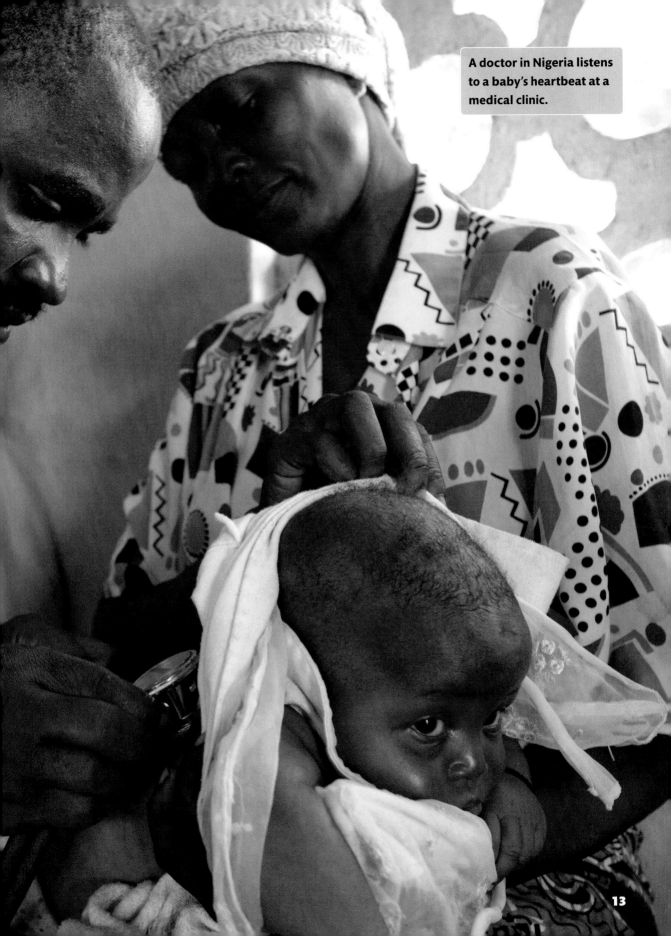

A doctor in Nigeria listens to a baby's heartbeat at a medical clinic.

HELP FROM THE HEALTH RANGERS

Governments throughout Africa have also taken action. For example, when the governor of Ondo State in Nigeria learned that maternal mortality was particularly bad in his region, he decided to act. With help from the World Bank, Governor Mimiko initiated the Abiye (a-bi-YAY) Safe Motherhood program. *Abiye* is a tribal word meaning "I will live and my child will live." The Abiye program enrolls all pregnant women, new mothers, and babies. Each woman is assigned a Health Ranger, who checks on her regularly. She also gets a mobile phone. Calls to her Health Ranger, the local hospital, or the governor himself with questions or concerns are free.

The Abiye program was launched in rural Ifedore (if-eh-DOH-reh), a part of Nigeria, in 2009. Right away, calls from mothers began pouring in. In the first 12 months of the program, 5,875 babies were delivered safely—an outstanding result. The number of births attended by trained **health personnel**, or professional health care providers, has increased greatly.

"If it were not for my Health Ranger and the doctor, I would have died."

—Justinah Chukwudi

A young woman meets with a nurse in Nigeria to learn about good health practices.

OTHER STEPS FOR NIGERIA'S CHILDREN

The Health Rangers are not the only story of hope. The World Health Organization (WHO), for example, has purchased nets to protect children and adults from disease-carrying mosquitoes. The UN is also educating Nigerian parents about nutrition. The organization is urging grocery stores to make sure they offer foods with essential nutrients.

Justinah Chukwudi, whom you read about earlier, was very happy that she enrolled in the Health Rangers program because her triplets were born healthy. "They saved my life and that of my children," she said. "If it were not for my Health Ranger and the doctor, I would have died."

Explore the Issue

1. **Identify Causes** What are the causes of poor health in children and mothers in Nigeria?

2. **Identify Problems and Solutions** How does the Abiye program address these health challenges?

15

Children's Nutrition in ROMAN

Nurses in Romania feed babies who are underweight at birth.

WHAT'S HAPPENING TO THE CHILDREN?

A few years ago, officials in Romania became concerned about a certain health issue. Statistics showed that Romanian children were smaller, on average, than children in other parts of Europe. Specifically, Romanian children between the ages of two and five were 21 percent shorter than children in the rest of the European Union.

Data also showed that Romanian children had more problems with health and development. Another startling statistic showed that Romanian babies usually weighed about 300 grams (or just over half a pound) less at birth than newborns elsewhere in Europe.

Simply, Romanian children were smaller and less healthy than other children in Europe. But the cause was not clear. Romania had been at peace with other countries since World War II. No major natural disasters, such as earthquakes or droughts, had harmed the food supply. People in Romania weren't starving. Yet something was threatening the health of Romania's children.

REDUCED TO POVERTY

About 22 million people live in the republic of Romania, a country of mountains, rolling hills, and fertile plains. The Danube, Europe's longest river, flows through the Romanian countryside for 600 miles. The country contains many natural gifts.

Romania was a prosperous country for much of its history. It began 4,000 years ago as the home of an ancient tribe called the Dacians. When the Romans conquered the Dacians, they gave Romania its name and the Latin roots of its language.

In spite of this early prosperity, though, Romania suffered after World War II. The postwar government was unstable. Right after the war, Romania was controlled by a military dictator. Power struggles continued over the next several decades. Government policies made Romania one of Europe's poorest countries. Citizens faced frequent shortages of food and fuel. In 2004, the average Romanian earned only about $4,485 a year. By comparison, a U.S. worker could earn more money in an hour than a Romanian could earn in an entire day.

ENOUGH TO EAT YET STARVING

Widespread poverty can hurt many aspects of a society, including the health of its people. Being poor doesn't automatically make someone unhealthy. However, poverty can lead to a poor diet, unclean living conditions, and a lack of medical care, all of which can cause ill health.

In Romania's case, poverty was hurting the children. They were smaller and sicker because of malnutrition. Malnutrition is not the same as hunger. A person who is hungry isn't getting enough to eat. A person who is malnourished isn't getting enough of the right nutrients, which are ingredients the body needs to grow and develop. Nutrients include vitamins, minerals, and protein.

Malnutrition can affect nearly every organ in the body. It can cause delayed, or **stunted**, growth, learning difficulties, and frequent infections. People of any age can be malnourished. In children, though, malnutrition is especially serious because it can cause permanent damage to bodies and minds.

OBSTACLES ON THE ROAD TO RECOVERY

Romania was a Communist dictatorship until 1989, when a violent revolution overthrew Romania's government and opened the way to reform. The country's fortunes have been getting better since.

Still, Romania remains very poor, and the reasons are complicated. About half of all Romanians live in rural areas. People outside the cities have less access to good food, clean water, and medical care. There aren't even enough farmers to manage the land. People live primarily on what they can grow themselves, which tends to be cabbage, potatoes, and beans.

As a result, the diets of many Romanian children are limited. Camelia Balan, who is an elementary school teacher, says, "You can see that their parents cannot afford to feed them properly. They cannot provide them with enough vegetables and fruits, and they can rarely give them meat." Another serious problem is that many thousands of Romanian children live in orphanages, and they also do not get enough milk, fruits, and vegetables.

KEY NUTRIENTS IN DIFFERENT FOODS

	CALCIUM	VITAMIN D	FIBER	POTASSIUM	PROTEIN	VITAMIN C	VITAMIN E	MAGNESIUM
Whole grains	✓		✓				✓	✓
Healthy fats and oils							✓	
Vegetables and fruits	✓		✓	✓	✓	✓	✓	✓
Nuts, seeds, beans, and tofu	✓		✓	✓	✓		✓	✓
Fish, poultry, meat, and eggs		✓			✓			✓
Dairy	✓	✓						

Source: Harvard University

A village in Romania receives fresh water during a major heat wave.

NEWBORN HEALTH

In 2001, the United Nations International Children's Emergency Fund (UNICEF) started a program that focused on newborn health. Romania was one of the countries UNICEF focused on for education. Through a program called the Baby Friendly Hospital Initiative, UNICEF has worked with maternity hospitals throughout Romania to educate new parents about proper care and nutrition for newborns. This focused approach improves the chances of infant survival and healthy child development.

Another effort has focused on replacing vitamins and minerals that are missing in the average Romanian diet. For example, foods that provide iodine, such as spinach or shellfish, are not readily available in Romania. The body needs iodine for a healthy **metabolism**, or body processes that sustain life. It is particularly important for pregnant women. Lack of iodine can also delay a child's growth and mental development. A new law in Romania now requires iodized salt in stores and bakeries.

GOOD NUTRITION AT SCHOOL

The Romanian government is working to help older children too. A few years ago, all schoolchildren began receiving free milk and a pastry at lunch to make sure they got enough calcium. More recently, Romania's Social Affairs Ministry pledged free vitamin tablets to all schoolchildren up to age 11.

Some Romanian people are approaching these changes cautiously. Others, though, agree with extra efforts to fight malnutrition in Romania. Among them are schoolteachers who see children in need.

"For most of the children in my classroom, receiving free vitamins would be a good thing," says Camelia Balan. Families, schools, and the government all need to be involved in improving the health of Romania's children. With a focus on good health care for babies and children, Romania can improve its health for generations to come.

Explore the Issue

1. **Analyze Cause and Effect** What are some factors that contributed to childhood malnutrition in Romania?

2. **Form and Support Opinions** Is education for new parents an effective way to improve childhood nutrition? Use information in the article to explain your answer.

Romanian children play outdoors in their village. Exercise and better nutrition are important for children's health.

Feliciano dos Santos

Sings Songs of Wellness

Santos, on the left, performs songs about washing hands, boiling water, and preventing disease, but he sings them in tribal languages to help get his message across.

HE'S THE GUITAR MAN

In a tiny community in southeast Africa, a world-renowned musician and his band tune up their guitars. A crowd gathers around them. As the band begins to play, everyone sways to the beat. Are the songs about love or fame or riches? Not exactly:

> Let's wash our hands
> Let's wash our hands
> For the children to stay healthy
> For the uncles to stay healthy
> For the mothers to stay healthy
> We build latrines
> —Feliciano dos Santos

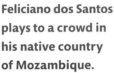

Feliciano dos Santos plays to a crowd in his native country of Mozambique.

This musician is more than a rock star. His name is Feliciano dos Santos, and he is a National Geographic Emerging Explorer on a mission to improve the health of Mozambique's poor.

Santos uses music to teach people how to fight disease that is spread through unclean water. His lyrics speak of simple things, such as washing hands. Yet his vision is big. Santos hopes to help his home country fight poverty by improving **sanitation**, the removal of trash and sewage to prevent disease. And he's succeeding. He is saving lives with songs.

EMERGING FROM POVERTY TO HOPE

National Geographic's Emerging Explorers Program supports the work of gifted young people who are committed to improving the world. As an Emerging Explorer, Santos has focused his efforts on a part of northern Mozambique called Niassa. This area is one of the poorest places on Earth—and it's where Santos was born and raised. More than 60 percent of Niassa's population is **illiterate**, meaning they cannot read or write. Few homes have running water. The average life expectancy is 42 years.

The World Health Organization estimates that unclean water and unsanitary conditions cause 80 percent of illness worldwide. As a child in Niassa, Santos caught polio from contaminated water. The disease left Santos partially disabled and determined to protect others in Niassa from the same fate.

THE POWER OF MUSIC TO HEAL

In 1977, a civil war broke out in Mozambique. It claimed close to a million lives and destroyed the country's economy. After the war, Santos wanted to help his home country heal. He started a band called Massukos. This word means "nourishing fruit." Music, he hoped, would help heal the mental wounds left by the war. The music of Massukos builds on the melodies, rhythms, and dialects of Niassa.

In time, Santos and his band became famous in Africa and even overseas. Yet Santos kept returning to Niassa. He still wanted to help the people there end poverty and illness. The region remains deeply poor.

SONGS AND SANITATION

In 2000, Santos started a nonprofit organization called Estamos. The mission of Estamos is to provide clean water throughout Niassa. The group helps provide water pumps plus low-cost, sustainable sanitation facilities.

The project is succeeding. Villagers have installed thousands of "EcoSan" portable bathrooms. The units are brick-lined to keep bacteria from leaking into the groundwater supply. The contents eventually become compost. After six months, the compost is a safe fertilizer for farmers to use in their fields. For the first time, Niassa is developing a sanitation system.

In addition, Santos is using music to teach people better **hygiene**, or keeping clean to prevent disease. One of Massukos's greatest hits is called "Tissambe Manja," or "Wash Our Hands." "Clean water is a basic human right, yet so many don't have it," says Santos. "I'm using my music to be the voice of people who have no voice."

Santos speaks to children about clean water.

Explore the Issue

1. **Analyze Causes** What are some of the factors contributing to Mozambique's low life expectancy?

2. **Identify Problems and Solutions** Why is Santos successful at teaching people about good health practices?

"I'm using my music to be the voice of people who have no voice."—Feliciano dos Santos

Santos writes songs in traditional melodies so people can remember the message even when the music is over.

Put On a Health Fair

A health fair is an event that includes displays and demonstrations about good health habits. You will be taking part in a health fair in your classroom or school to make people more aware of healthful practices. Who knows? You might add years to people's lives—and life to their years!

IDENTIFY

- Find out what some of the health issues are in your community. Ask friends, family, and neighbors what they think are important practices in daily life that keep them healthy.

- Identify the gaps. What else is important for good health in your community?

- Work with three or four classmates. Prepare to do research and take part in a health fair in your classroom or school.

RESEARCH

- For the health fair, your group will have a booth to present information about a healthful habit. For example, regular exercise is a healthful habit.

- Begin by deciding what healthful habit to present. Another example might be to show how to prepare a healthful meal.

- Use library resources or the Internet to collect information.

Students in Florida do jumping jacks as part of an exercise campaign.

ORGANIZE

- Plan how you will create your booth and present your information in an interesting way.

- Create a visual display that shows the healthful habit. The display could be a poster, or you could even use presentation software.

- Include a demonstration. For example, one member of your group could demonstrate simple ways to build exercise into daily life.

SHARE

- On the day of the health fair, set up your booth and prepare for your demonstration.

- As visitors come to your booth, greet them politely. Then show them your visual display and present your demonstration.

- Ask visitors whether they have any questions and provide thorough answers.

- Take photos or make a video as a record of your presentation.

Write a
TV News Story

Discoveries that improve human health are happening all the time. Some involve advanced technology. Others do not. Some of the most important breakthroughs in health have come from using everyday things in new ways.

What are some of these discoveries? Why are they effective? Your assignment is to research and write a script for a TV news story. The story should inform your audience about one low-cost, high-impact discovery that is improving people's health care.

RESEARCH

Use the Internet, books, and articles to research and answer the following questions:

- Why is this discovery important? Use facts to explain who is affected by it and how.
- How is this discovery similar to or different from other discoveries in this field? What makes it unique and newsworthy?
- Who are the experts in this field? What do they think?

DRAFT

Review your notes and write a first draft of the script.

- Start with a statement that introduces your topic clearly and previews what is to follow. Explain why you're reporting about the story from your location. Think about sharing a story or presenting an interesting fact to illustrate the discovery and engage the listener.
- The body of your script should use relevant facts, definitions, and concrete details. It should also include quotations and other information and examples. In addition, use interviews to explain why this discovery matters.
- The conclusion should follow from and support the information presented in the body of the script. Explain how this discovery could affect the listener and why it matters.

REVISE & EDIT

Read your script aloud to make sure it's interesting and clear.

- Does the introduction clearly identify the discovery? Does it capture the listener's attention?
- Does the body of the script include facts to inform your audience about the discovery and its potential?
- Does the script end with a conclusion that makes sense based on the facts and interviews?
- What idea will your listeners take away from the news story? Be sure that this is the most important idea.

Be sure to recheck all your facts and the spelling of all the words in your script to be sure everything is correct.

PUBLISH & PRESENT

Practice delivering your script as if you were a TV news reporter. What visuals or interviews would you include? Then record yourself. Ask for permission to "air" your news story by emailing it to family and friends or by sharing it through your school's media center.

Visual GLOSSARY

developing nation *n.*, a nation with a low income per person

GDP per capita *n.*, an estimation of the value of goods produced by each person in a country

health care *n.*, medical services

health personnel *n.*, professional health care providers

heredity *n.*, the passing of genes from one generation to the next

hygiene *n.*, the practice of keeping clean to prevent disease

illiterate *adj.*, unable to read or write

life expectancy *n.*, the average number of years a person can expect to live

malaria *n.*, a disease carried by mosquitoes

malnutrition *n.*, a lack of nourishing food

metabolism *n.*, body processes that sustain life

nutrient *n.*, an ingredient, such as a vitamin, mineral, or protein, that the body needs to grow and develop

sanitation *n.*, the removal of trash and sewage to prevent disease

stunted *adj.*, delayed or stopped, as in growth or development

virus *n.*, a tiny organism that infects living cells with disease

heredity

hygiene

health care

virus

malaria

31

INDEX

SKILLS